Children of the World

Mexico

For their help in the preparation of *Children of the World: Mexico*, the editors gratefully thank Nicolas Escalante, Embassy of Mexico (Canada), Ottawa; William Jarrett, the Center for Latin America, University of Wisconsin - Milwaukee; Gloria Jimenez and Filiberto Murguia, the Spanish Center, Milwaukee; Armando Rios, Milwaukee, Wis.; Rita Tenorio, the Milwaukee Public Schools; and Carlos Tujalte, Embassy of Mexico (US), Washington, DC.

British Library Cataloguing in Publication Data

Mexico.
1. Mexico. Social life
I. Ikuhara, Yoshiyuki II. Knowlton, MaryLee, 1946 -
III. Sachner, Mark J. 1948 - IIII. Series
954.9'6

ISBN 0-83687-072-7

This UK edition first published in 1989 by
Gareth Stevens Children's Books
31 Newington Green, London N16 9PU

This work was originally published in shortened form consisting of Section 1 only.

Editor (UK): John O'Brien
Map design: Gary Moseley

1 2 3 4 5 6 7 8 9 95 94 93 92 91 90 89

Printed in the United States of America

Children of the World
Mexico

Photography by
Yoshiyuki Ikuhara

Edited by
MaryLee Knowlton &
Mark J. Sachner

Gareth Stevens Children's Books
LONDON • MILWAUKEE

. . . a note about *Children of the World*:

The children of the world live in fishing towns and urban centres, on islands and in mountain valleys, on sheep ranches and fruit farms. This series follows one child in each country through the pattern of his or her life. Candid photographs show the children with their families, at school, at play, and in their communities. The text describes the dreams of the children and, often through their own words, tells how they see themselves and their lives.

Each book also explores events that are unique to the country in which the child lives, including festivals, religious ceremonies, and national holidays. The *Children of the World* series does more than tell about foreign countries. It introduces the children of each country and shows readers what it is like to be a child in that country.

. . . and about *Mexico*:

Maria Elena lives in Guadalajara, Mexico's second largest city, with her parents and two young sisters. Her family's modest success allows her to enjoy the diversity of life in a city both ancient and modern. Elena's many interests keep her busy from morning until night at school, in the markets, and at a variety of religious and other festivals and celebrations.

To enhance this book's value in libraries and classrooms, comprehensive reference sections include up-to-date data about Mexico's geography, demographics, language, currency, education, culture, industry, and natural resources. *Mexico* also features a bibliography, research topics, activity projects, and discussions of such subjects as Mexico City, the country's history, political system, ethnic and religious composition, and immigrants to Canada and the US.

The living conditions and experiences of children in Mexico vary tremendously according to economic, environmental, and ethnic situations. The reference sections help bring to life for young readers the diversity and richness of the culture and heritage of Mexico.

CONTENTS

LIVING IN MEXICO:
Maria Elena, a Girl from the City

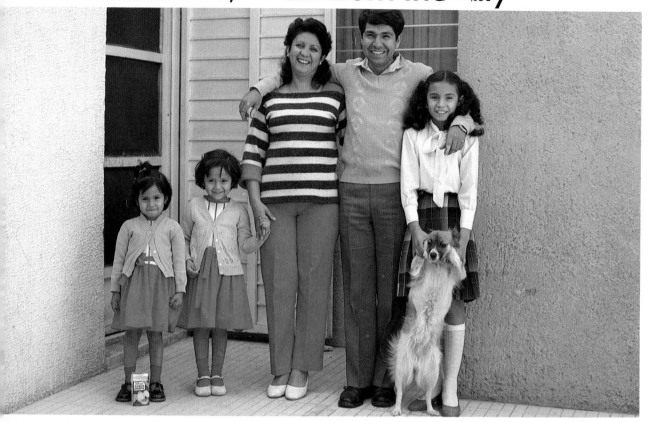

¡Hola! yo soy Maria Elena Manzo Rios

'Hello! I'm Maria Elena Manzo Rios'.

Elena is a ten-year-old girl from Mexico, the land of the sun. She lives with her father, Francisco; her mother, also named Elena; and her two sisters, five-year-old Christina and three-year-old Isabel. They are a Roman Catholic family. More than 95% of all Mexicans are Catholic.

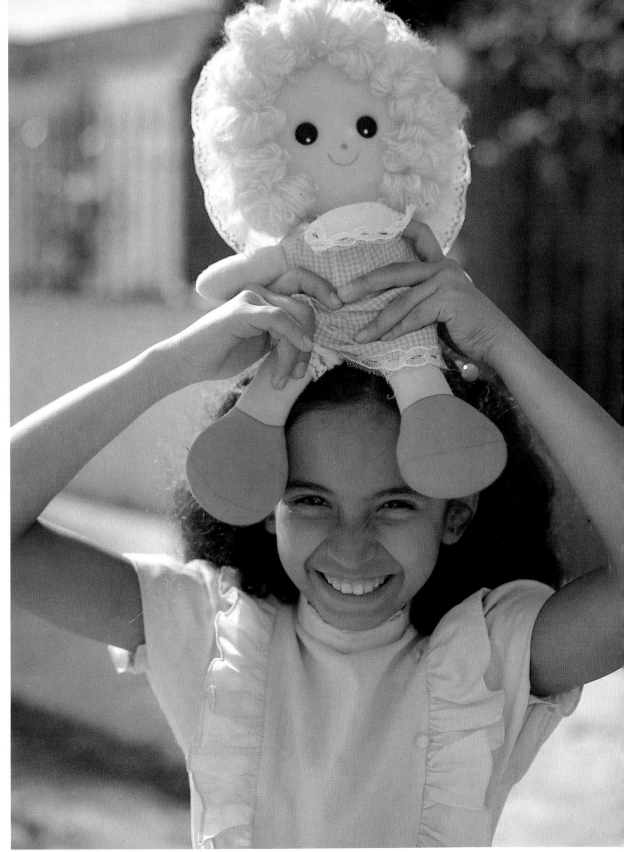

'My doll Rosita was a present from *Mamá Grande*, my grandmother'.

Guadalajara, Elena's Home Town

Elena and her family live in Guadalajara, the second largest city in Mexico. It is also the capital of the state of Jalisco. The city was built in 1542 by the Spanish. Today it is home to more than 3 million people.

Guadalajara is a lively mixture of both old and new. As a major Mexican city, it is a centre of business and industry. However, many historical buildings, such as the Cathedral and its four surrounding plazas, the Degollado Theatre, and the Basilica de Zapopan, remain from its earliest days when Spain ruled the country.

Basilica de Zapopan. Worshippers kneel on the stone road to pray.

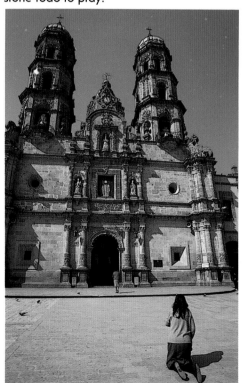

Colourful Christmas decorations stay up until after Epiphany.

In the northern part of the city is the Cabañas Orphanage, built in 1830. The mural by José Clement Orozco in the dome of its chapel is very famous. It is very high. To see it, you must either look straight up or use a mirror to reflect it.

Degollado Theatre. Many plays and concerts are performed here.

Christmas decorations in Liberation Plaza.

Inside the Basilica de Zapopan.

The main street of Guadalajara is Juárez Avenue. Mexicans also call it the Avenue of September 16. September 16 is Mexican Independence Day. Parades are held along this avenue on Christmas and Mexican Independence Day each year.

In the centre of the city is the Libertad Market. Here, about 4,000 small shops sell everything from food and household goods to folk crafts. The world-famous Mexican pottery and glass are popular with foreign visitors.

Guadalajara is a long way from the sea and 1,553 m above sea level. During the rainy season of June and July, it rains for a while every day. For the rest of the year, the climate is very mild and pleasant.

Like Elena and her sisters, both of their parents were born and raised in Guadalajara. They are all of mixed Spanish and Indian heritage, or *mestizo*.

Juárez Avenue is the busiest street in Guadalajara.
There are no bus stops; the buses stop when people raise their hands.

A market in the centre of Guadalajara.

Cooking and Eating

The staple food of the Mexican diet is the *tortilla*, a kind of crepe made of corn flour. The tortilla is like bread in our diet. When the tortilla is dried and fried in oil, it is called a *tostada*. Tortillas are eaten with soup, meat, or vegetables. When beans, tomatoes, chilies, avocados, and sometimes meat are added, a tortilla becomes a *taco*!

Elena's favourite food is *carne en su jugo*, a dish resembling a beef and onion soup. Her mother promises, 'If you do well on the next sewing test, I will make carne soup and quesadillas'. Elena loves *quesadillas*. Most of you would, too, because they are a lot like cheese pizza!

An endless variety of chilies, peas, and beans.

Tortilla, the staple food of Mexico.

Cactus and *guanges*, a type of pea.

Street vendors sell cooked food.

Some say there are 4,000 types of traditional cooking in Mexico! Corn and beans have been grown here for thousands of years. But most people think of hot chili peppers when they think of Mexican food. Indeed, Mexico has many kinds of chilies. Chilies give a strong flavour to food, and they are full of vitamins. Elena's father loves chili sauce and pours it over most of his food.

Thanks to Guadalajara's mild climate, fruit grows in great quantities, and juices are sold on the street by vendors. In poor sections of the cities and villages, most food is sold by street vendors. Many customers cannot afford refrigerators. They must buy their food freshly picked or butchered each day.

The tap water is not good, so people buy bottled water for drinking and cooking. Every day trucks come with bottled water to sell.

A shop sign in Tlaquepaque.

Red glassware called *sangre de pichón* (pigeon blood).

Folk crafts.

Shopping in Tlaquepaque

Elena goes shopping with her mother to Tlaquepaque, about ten minutes by bus from home. Tlaquepaque is a shopping town. It is known for pottery, hand-blown glass, and many other kinds of handicrafts. Elena and her mother have come here to buy a birthday present for Elena's father.

Elena and her mother in Tlaquepaque.

Mariachi musicians.

Tlaquepaque is also known as the home of *mariachi* music. These strolling musicians are called *mariachis*. They are popular in larger cities like Guadalajara and Mexico City, as well as in tourist areas such as Tlaquepaque.

The mariachis play many kinds of music. Elena's favourite songs are *corridos*, which are long, rhymed verses with witty words and simple tunes. Elena's mother tells her that she and Francisco used to come to Tlaquepaque when they were dating. Today Elena enjoys hearing the songs her parents have often told her about.

Elena's house. Workers are building a second-story addition.

At Home with Elena's Family

Elena's home is in a new residential area twelve minutes by car from Guadalajara city centre. Nearby is an industrial area with many cement factories and oil refineries. Elena's parents bought this house nine years ago. It has three bedrooms, a living room, and a kitchen.

Most of the houses in the neighbourhood have dogs, since there have been some robberies. Elena has a dog named Canelita, a gift from her grandmother.

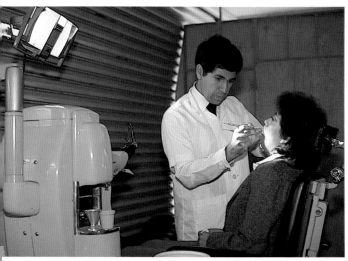

Elena's father at work.

Elena's father, Francisco, is a dentist. When he was just twelve, he began working as an assistant to a dentist. After graduating from dental school, he opened up a dental clinic in an area where many poorer people live.

Mexicans do not often go to the dentist even when they have a toothache, in part because so many of them are very poor. Elena's father provides low-cost dental care to poor people.

Elena and her family relax at home.

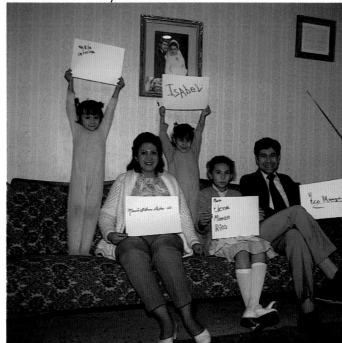

Elena's family eats all their meals together. Breakfast is at 7 a.m., and for Elena it is a very light meal, usually just milk and a biscuit. After breakfast her father takes all the children to school on his way to work.

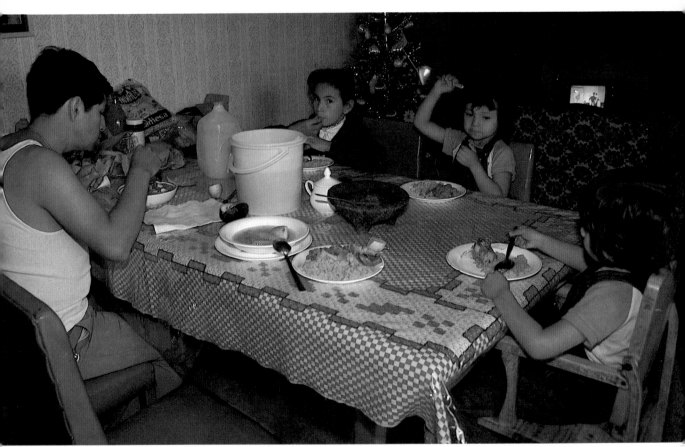

Lunch is the main meal of the day.

After school he brings them home for lunch, the main meal of the day. After lunch, people take a *siesta*, or nap. Most children don't sleep, but grown-ups do. After siesta, Francisco goes back to work. Elena washes dishes before she does her school homework. Cristina and Isabel play together, one moment quarrelling and crying, and the next moment laughing together.

Dinner is the happiest time of the day for Elena. Although it is a very light meal, it is a time for families. Everyone at the table talks about their day's events.

At supper everyone enjoys talking about the events of the day.

Elena loves to talk about her friends and her school. Often she tells stories she has made up to entertain Christina and Isabel. Her parents enjoy talking and listening to each other and their children at this peaceful time of the day.

Mexico's Second Christmas

Today is January 6, the Feast of Epiphany *(Los Santos Reyes)*. In Mexico children get presents at Epiphany in memory of the gifts presented by the Three Wise Men to the baby Jesus. It's like a second Christmas for the children of Mexico. The day begins with a church service in the morning.

The holiday begins with a church service. The sermon seems longer than usual.

Cutting the *rosca de reyes*. Who will get the baby doll baked inside?

Blindfolded, Elena tries to break the piñata.

Elena and her father dance for their guests.

After church, the children of neighbours and relatives arrive for the festivities. A large pot called a *piñata* contains fruit and sweets. The blindfolded children take turns trying to break the piñata with a stick. The piñata hangs on a string and swings back and forth, so it's not easy to break. Once it breaks everybody scrambles for the treats.

A high point of the party for Elena is dancing with her father. He has taught her all kinds of steps, and both of them are skilled dancers.

Elena helps her mother with the cleaning.

Working and Playing at Home

Elena has made three promises to her mother: to do things on her own, to look after her younger sisters, and to help her mother with housework. Since her sisters are still very little, they are not much help with the housework. Elena sometimes wishes she had older brothers or sisters to share the load and to play with.

Today Elena has done some cleaning and washing. She hangs out all the washing on the upstairs veranda. She will leave it there until it dries, rain or shine.

Hanging the clothes on the upstairs veranda.

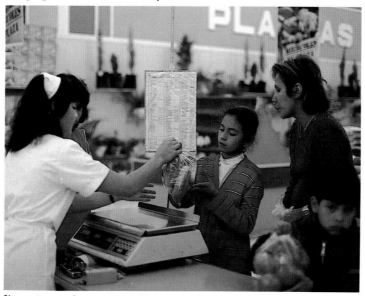

Shopping at the supermarket.

The hardest promise to keep is to look after her sisters. They often do not obey her, and they cry if she gets angry with them. Then Elena gets scolded!

Being the oldest child can be very hard because it means having many responsibilities. But Elena's parents reward her for her help at home. They take her with them for special outings, and she feels that it all evens out.

Elena loves to read. Her favourite magazine is a weekly comic called 'Capulinita'. She buys it with her pocket money, her 'mi domingo', which is 100 pesos a week.

She also loves to read stories and fairy tales. She wants to write children's stories when she grows up. She writes her stories in a notebook and illustrates them with her own drawings. When she thinks she has a story just the way she wants it, she reads it to her sisters.

Elena will be in junior high school next September. To enter junior high, students must take an entrance examination. Elena has already begun studying for it.

All children must attend primary school. Most choose to go on to high school, but some do not. Some families are so poor that the children must go to work right after primary school. Other children get married very young. In Mexico, a boy can marry at sixteen and a girl at thirteen if they have their parents' permission.

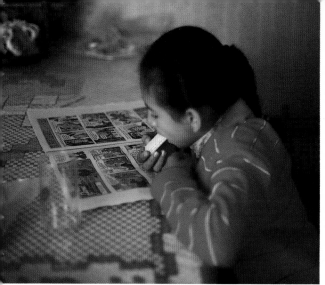

Reading comics, an after-school pleasure.

Watching TV after homework.

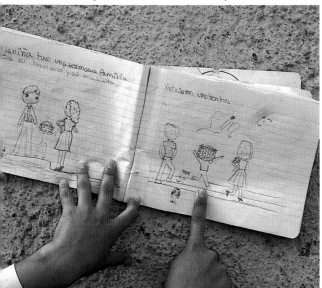

An illustrated story created by Elena.

Isabel wants someone to play with her.

Homework.

Elena washes before she goes to bed. And she *always* brushes her teeth.

Elena has a lot of school homework. She knows she must study hard to prepare for her writing career. When school is out, she does her homework before she does anything else. Then she reads comics or watches TV. Her favourite programme is 'My Clever Dog Joy', because the little dog reminds her of her own dog, Canelita.

A slumber party with Lupe. Lots of giggling, not much sleeping.

Today Elena's cousin Lupe is coming to stay overnight. For fun, all the children sleep in the same bed. They need only one blanket over them, since even at night it is warm all year long.

Going to school.

Elena and Her Friends at School

In Mexico there is a big gap between the rich and the poor. Elena's family is considered to be well-off. They can afford the children's education as well as a TV set and two cars. Elena knows she is very lucky. Her father's work among poorer people has made her aware of other people's hardship.

Elena goes to Lucio Blanco Urbana School Número 49. The building is 400 years old but has only been used as a school since 1930. It is in the middle of town, and children commute from all over the city.

The school classes are given in three sessions: 8 a.m. to 1 p.m., 2 p.m. to 6:30 p.m. and 7 p.m. to 9 p.m. The evening session is for those over fifteen years of age who did not finish primary school when they were young. It has pupils of all ages.

Textbooks.

Elena is ten years old and would normally be in the sixth year. But she skipped the first year, so she is in the seventh year. Her class has 37 students. Students cannot go on to the next year if they miss school often or if they don't pass their courses. So Elena's class has students from ten to fifteen years of age.

The students all have to study the national language, Spanish, and mathematics, science, social studies, art, sewing, health, and physical education. They study two subjects a day. Since there are no school grounds or gym, they usually practise marching for ceremonies during physical education classes. Elena is good at Spanish and social studies, but not at sewing.

It's Friday, and an outdoor market is held in front of the school.

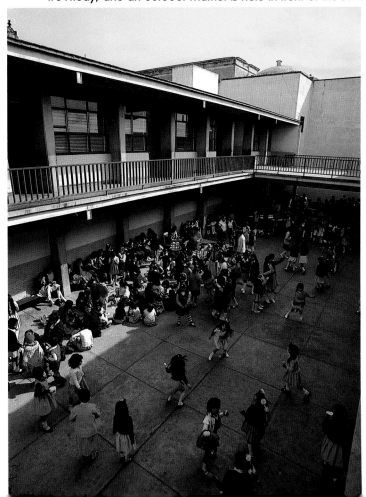

The school courtyard during break.

Elena and her classmates.

Sewing class. Elena's improving!

Elena recites her homework for the class.

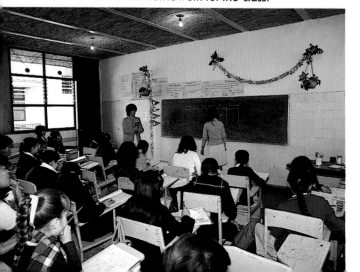

One more hour until break!

The teacher's son comes to school with her today.

Today Elena's teacher has brought her two-year-old son, José, to school. The girls take turns looking after him. The students are quite free, even during class time. They talk to each other or even do knitting.

Mrs Luze-Casillas, the head teacher.

The girls play with their dolls during break.

The students salute the national flag.

The national flag ceremony.

During the class break, the girls play house and other games in the school courtyard. Some may not have eaten breakfast at home, and they catch up by munching bread.

The students practise once a month for the Independence Day and National Flag Day parades. The ceremonies have a different theme every month. This month the theme is 'World Friendship'. The lower years wear the national costumes of different countries. The upper years march and practise a flag-raising ceremony.

The children dress in the costumes of many nations to promote world friendship.

The younger boys dress up as cowboys.

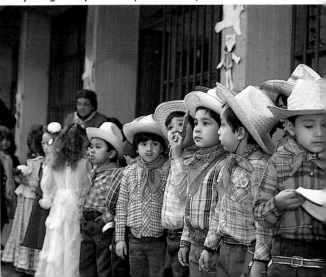

School's Out!

After school the students all go home. Many students in Mexican schools are from poor families. They must get jobs when they are very young, so there are no school clubs or after-school activities. Elena and her sisters go to her grandmother's house, and their father picks them up for lunch.

Elena plays a hopscotch game with the girls in her neighbourhood. It is called *'bebeleche'*. The boys play soccer or play with their tops or marbles.

Usually boys and girls don't play together. Moral education at home is very strict, especially for girls. Boys dream of becoming *matadors*, bullfighters. Every girl looks forward to her fifteenth birthday, when she wears a very special dress and is recognized as an adult.

Playing hopscotch.

Waiting for their father at Grandmother's house. Two of the little children are the brother and sister of Elena's father. Elena is older than her aunt and uncle.

43

At the supermarket.

Mexico is said to be the birth-place of cocoa. Elena loves many Mexican chocolate sweets, such as a chocolate layer cake called *Gansito* and a chocolate-coated jelly sweet called *Submarino*.

The Wall Market changes locations every day. Every Wednesday it opens in front of Elena's house. People can buy everything from household goods and food to traditional Indian medicine. On other days Elena's family shops in a supermarket near their house. Many supermarket goods come from the United States.

Mexican sweets.

The sweet turns Elena's tongue red.

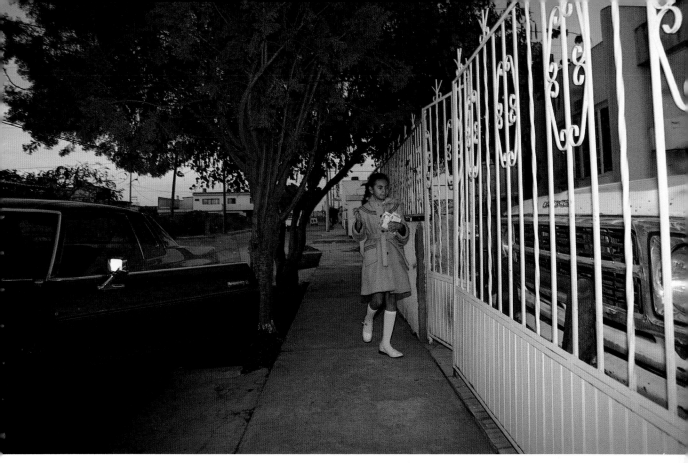

Walking home from the market.

Elena's had a long, full day, and she's tired.

Swimming with Lupe.

A Birthday Weekend

Every year Elena's family spends a weekend at the Guadalajara University Sports Club to celebrate her father's birthday. The club is like a resort hotel with all kinds of sports and games.

This year, because she has been so helpful at home, Elena gets to bring her cousin Lupe along. As soon as they arrive, Elena and Lupe change into bathing suits and jump into the pool. Living so far from the sea, the girls don't often get to swim. This is a treat they will talk about until next year.

In the evening the family throws a birthday party at the club. All their friends and relatives are there. Until the early hours of the morning, they eat, drink, sing, and dance. The children get to stay up as long as they can stay awake.

Everybody dances at the birthday party!

Maria Elena says '¡Adios!' She hopes you will learn Spanish so that someday you can read the books she is going to write. '¡Hasta la vista!'

FOR YOUR INFORMATION: Mexico

Official name:
Estados Unidos Mexicanos
(es-TAH-dos u-NEE-dos meh-hee-CAN-os)

Capital:
Mexico City

United States of Mexico

Many old ruins survive at Teotihuacán.

History

The Indian Nations

In ancient times Mexico was first a hunting and gathering society. It was then a farming society. The earliest villages appeared around 2000 BC, or about 4,000 years ago. The Spanish invaded Mexico in the sixteenth century. Up to that time, the history of Mexico is the history of the Indians.

Olmecs: About 200 BC the Olmecs built a city near what is now Veracruz. Historical remains have been found in the ruins of La Venta. These remains include earthenware, clay figures, and huge stone sculptures of human faces.

Mexica: A large religious city appeared in the Central Plateau between 300 BC and AD 750. The city was named Teotihuacán. This means 'City of the Gods'. The largest remains of this city are near Mexico City. These remains include the Pyramid of the Sun. It is 65.5 m high. Its volume is greater than any of the pyramids of Egypt.

Mayans: The Mayans originated in the jungles of Guatemala. In 100 BC, they had a highly developed society in the Yucatán Peninsula. Hieroglyphic records of their rule survive. The Mayans developed a very accurate calendar. It shows only a 0.0002 day difference from the solar calendar calculated by modern astronomers. The Mayan civilization survived until AD 900.

Aztecs: The last great Indian empire was that created by the Aztecs. It appeared about AD 1200. The Aztec capital was Tenochtitlán, at the site of present-day Mexico City. Spain invaded the area 300 years later. At that time, Tenochtitlán was probably the largest city in the world. The Spaniards left records that detail the size of the city and its great beauty. After describing its beauty, they then destroyed most of it. The last remains of the floating gardens of the Aztec princes are in Xochimilco. Today Aztec boatmen pole tourists around the park's islands in flower-covered boats.

Colonial Period

In 1519 Hernán Cortés landed on the eastern shore of Mexico. With him were 315 Spanish soldiers. The Aztec emperor Montezuma welcomed the light-skinned foreigners and treated them as honoured guests.

Within two years of landing, the Spanish had betrayed the Aztecs. They took over the government and destroyed the city. The land was given to Spanish governors. They built huge estates or farms, called *haciendas,* which they ran with Indian slave labour. The Catholic Church and the Spanish government shared the great wealth from Mexico's silver and gold mines. The Spanish brought European diseases like smallpox, and epidemics killed many of the natives.

War of Independence and the Mexican-American War

In 1810 began the war of independence from Spain. On 16 September, Father Miguel Hidalgo, a small-town priest, rang the church bell, shouting 'Viva Mexico'! Each 16 September, the nation celebrates Independence Day. In 1821, after much fighting, the people established the Empire of Mexico. Years of war and unrest followed the declaration of independence. From 1846 to 1848, the United States and Mexico fought a war over Texas. Mexico suffered repeated defeats in battle. These defeats resulted in the loss of Texas, Arizona, and California. This land made up half of Mexico's original territory.

Pyramid of the Sun at Teotihuacán.

A plaza near modern Xochimilco.

Xochimilco — the 'Venice of Mexico'.

Revolution and Reform

By 1863, Mexico was bankrupt and in 1864 agreed to be ruled by an Austrian emperor backed by France. The Mexican army, however, fought for freedom. In 1867 they defeated the French. Once again, Mexico was free under President Benito Juárez. Juárez, an Indian, was a just ruler who had been driven out of power by the French. In 1876, shortly after his death, Porfirio Díaz seized power and ruled as dictator. He restored order, but denied liberty and land to Indians and the poor. His 34-year rule set the stage for the Mexican Revolution.

The Mexican Revolution

The revolution of 1910 had many heroes. Francisco (Panchito) Madero was the first president following Díaz. Pancho Villa was a former bandit and rebel leader in the north. And Emiliano Zapata was a peasant leader from the south. Although these heroes were assassinated, all three survived in stories and song.

Chaos and coups dominated Mexico until 1917. That was the year a progressive constitution was set up. This was a major step toward modernization. The revolution cost over a million lives and caused terrible destruction. One out of every eight Mexicans died as a result of the revolution. But it became the basis for Mexican pride and identity as a nation. The revolution meant equal rights and opportunity for all Mexicans. These values are the cornerstone of Mexican government.

Population and Ethnic Groups

The Mexican population (about 80,000,000) is made up of three groups: Indian, 30%; Spanish, 10%; and mixed Indian and Spanish blood, called *mestizo*, 60%. Many of the pureblooded Indians live in mountain regions. There, they keep their traditional languages and customs.

Language

Spanish is the national language of Mexico, but over 50 native Indian languages are also still spoken. Spanish is the language of the schools, however. The government's goal is to teach every child to read and write Spanish.

Religion

More than 95% of Mexicans are Roman Catholic. Catholicism is often mixed with native Indian religion, however, especially for fiestas and for tourists. Unlike many other Christian colonies, Mexico has been tolerant of native beliefs and practices.

Education

Until the revolution, all education was private and the country was largely illiterate. Only the wealthy could attend schools. Mexico now devotes much attention, energy, and money to educating its people. Its literacy rate is now 74%. This means that three out of four adults can read.

Poverty continues to have an effect on Mexican education. Although the government attempts to provide at least ten years of school, many children cannot take advantage of it. Instead, at a very young age they must contribute to the family income. This means that children must learn the skills and handicrafts of their parents. As a result, fewer than 10% of children between 11 and 15 attend school.

One-third of Mexico's budget goes to education. This figure is much higher than in most countries. This may be why the government has so successfully educated its people, despite the rapidly increasing population and variety of complex Indian languages.

Because there are so few teachers, about half the rural schools teach only the first three years. Some rural schools teach farming techniques to children who will become farmers. Often adults from the area attend to learn more modern ways of farming.

Boys and girls do not attend school together in Mexico. They have separate play-grounds and wings of the school. Sometimes they take part in programmes together. Even then, however, they take part in different parts of the programme and do not have much contact. They study some of the same things, like Spanish, history, arithmetic, and religion. Often, however, the girls study home-related topics like sewing and cooking, while the boys study science and government. These and other courses are designed to prepare boys for further education and careers.

Mexico is home to the oldest university in all the Americas. The National University of Mexico was founded in 1551 in Mexico City. Today it has over 100,000 students. In 1950, the University was expanded and more than 80 new buildings were built. It is now known as University City. During over 300 years of Spanish rule, the university granted 40,000 degrees. But they were granted only to students wealthy enough to attend. Today education is free for all Mexicans, and children study hard in school so a university education can be part of their future.

Art and Music

At the time of the revolution in 1910, three-quarters of Mexican adults could not read. The Ministry of Public Education and Fine Arts hired artists to create art that would educate and inspire the people. Jóse Clemente Orozco, Diego Rivera, and David Alfaro Siqueiros are three great painters. Their art portrays the causes of the Mexican Revolution. Their murals in many public buildings and museums are famous for the way they show Mexican history and culture. Their style is truly Mexican.

Music played with European instruments but with Indian and Spanish influences is very popular in Mexico. *Trio, mariachi,* and *marimbas* music is often said to express the heart of the Mexican people. A dance called the *Jarabe Tapitio* from the state of Jalisco is the national folkloric dance. Each region of Mexico has music and dances that are special to the people of that region. Mexicans value the variety and liveliness of their folk arts.

Sports

Mexico's most popular sport is soccer, which Mexicans call *fútbol*. In June, 1986, Mexico played host to the World Cup soccer tournament. · The major site for the games was Aztec Stadium, which seats 110,000 people. Aztec Stadium is in Mexico City, which sits in a mountain valley 2.1 km above sea level. People who are not used to such a high altitude often must become used to breathing Mexico City's rather thin — polluted — air. The air can make playing difficult for foreign teams.

Also popular in Mexico is *jai-alai*, or *pelota*. This game, which is like handball, comes from the Basque region of Spain. Jai-alai is the fastest ball game in the world. Spain is the source of another popular sport — bullfighting. The Plaza in Mexico City is the world's largest bullring. Other popular sports imports include baseball and basketball from the United States.

Mexicans are known for their excellent horsemanship. They compete in rodeos, known as *charreados*. Riders wear Mexican *charro* costumes decorated with gold and silver. The famous *sombrero* with its large brim tops off the outfit.

Agriculture

About 33% of the labour force in Mexico is made up of farmers. Their main crops are corn, coffee, sugar cane, cotton, and vegetables. Mexican land is rich, but the rough ground and lack of rainfall make it hard for small landowners to grow their crops. By the year 2000, only 18% of Mexico's labour force is expected to be made up of farmers.

Under Spanish rule, most of the farming land had been owned by wealthy Spaniards. Indian slaves, or *peons*, provided the labour. After the Revolution, the government broke up the haciendas and redistributed the land more fairly.

Today 12% of the land is used for agriculture. The government provides water for much of this land by irrigating it. But because the plots of land are very small, farming is a hard and sometimes unprofitable business. During the winter months, there may be no work at all in the north. This is when thousands of northern farmers leave and work as illegal aliens in the US. They return home for the spring and summer to work in the fields. Also, more farmers are moving with their families to the cities. There, they join the ranks of the unemployed living in shanty towns.

Times are hard now, but the government is determined to improve farm production. Many programmes have been developed that have done much already. Deserts and jungles have been turned into productive farms and ranches. Education programmes have helped isolated farms modernize their methods.

Land

The area of Mexico is 1,225,421 sq km. This area makes Mexico about five times larger than the UK. Three-quarters of Mexico is a high plateau, between 1,500-2,400 m above sea level. This plateau is between two mountain ranges, the Eastern (*Oriental*) and Western (*Occidental*) Sierra Madres. On the coastal sides of the mountain ranges, rich plains lead to the seas. The land of Mexico varies greatly. It ranges from snowy mountains and volcanoes to tropical forests and deserts. It has shores to the Pacific Ocean, the Caribbean Sea, and the Gulf of Mexico.

Climate

Mexico is divided into five climatic zones — tropical, temperate, cool, plateau, and ice. Along the plains of the seacoast it is possible to swim all year long. Many of the major cities, such as Mexico City and Guadalajara, are in the Central Plateau region in the middle of the country. They have mild weather year-round.

Natural Resources

Mexico is rich in minerals. Long ago, these minerals were exploited by foreign-owned companies. Now Mexicans control each company that mines.

Mexico produces 25% of the world's silver. This makes Mexico the world's leading silver producer. Mexico also has what may well be the world's largest supply of oil reserves. This makes oil Mexico's leading export. Based on its large supply of oil, Mexico borrowed money from international banks. It used this money to develop industry and social programmes in the 1970s. The falling prices of oil have now made it hard for Mexico to meet its debts. As profits from the oil industry have gone down, unemployment and poverty have gone up. In addition to oil and silver, Mexico exports copper, gold, lead, zinc, natural gas, and timber to other countries.

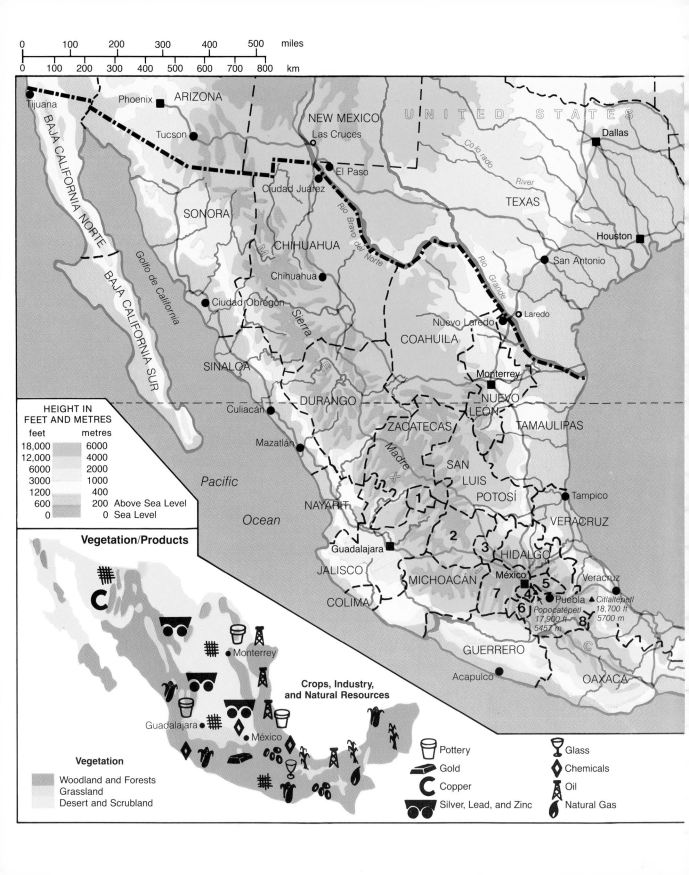

miles
0   100   200   300   400   500

km
0   100   200   300   400   500   600   700   800

Tijuana
BAJA CALIFORNIA NORTE
BAJA CALIFORNIA SUR
Golfo de California

Phoenix
ARIZONA
Tucson
NEW MEXICO
Las Cruces
El Paso
Ciudad Juárez
SONORA
CHIHUAHUA
Chihuahua
Ciudad Obregón
Sierra

UNITED STATES
Colorado
River
Dallas
TEXAS
Houston
San Antonio
Rio Bravo del Norte
Rio Grande
Nuevo Laredo
Laredo
COAHUILA
Monterrey
NUEVO LEÓN
TAMAULIPAS

HEIGHT IN FEET AND METRES

feet	metres	
18,000	6000	
12,000	4000	
6000	2000	
3000	1000	
1200	400	
600	200	Above Sea Level
0	0	Sea Level

SINALOA
Culiacán
Mazatlán
DURANGO
ZACATECAS
SAN LUIS POTOSÍ
Madre
Tampico
VERACRUZ

Pacific
Ocean
NAYARIT
Guadalajara
JALISCO
COLIMA
MICHOACÁN
1
2
3
HIDALGO
México
7
5
4
Puebla
6
Popocatépetl
17,900 ft
5457 m
Veracruz
Citlaltépetl
18,700 ft
5700 m
8
GUERRERO
Acapulco
OAXACA

Vegetation/Products

Monterrey
Guadalajara
México

Crops, Industry, and Natural Resources

Vegetation

- Woodland and Forests
- Grassland
- Desert and Scrubland

Pottery
Gold
Copper
Silver, Lead, and Zinc

Glass
Chemicals
Oil
Natural Gas

MEXICO — Political and Physical

ARKANSAS

MISSISSIPPI

Birmingham

Columbus

GEORGIA

Atlantic
Ocean

LOUISIANA

Jackson

ALABAMA

Baton Rouge

Jacksonville

New Orleans

FLORIDA

Tampa

Mississippi River

THE
BAHAMAS

Gulf
of
Mexico

Miami

Nassau

Tropic of Cancer

Havana

CUBA

Guantánamo

Canal
de
Yucatán

Mérida

Golfo
de
Campeche

YUCATÁN

Caribbean   Sea

JAMAICA

Kingston

CAMPECHE

QUINTANA
ROO

TABASCO

Belize

Golfo de Honduras

BELIZE

CHIAPAS

Tapachula

GUATEMALA

Guatemala

HONDURAS

Tegucigalpa

San
Salvador

EL
SALVADOR

NICARAGUA

Managua

Corn
Coffee
Textiles
Sugar Cane

GENERAL REFERENCE

Countries	States
MEXICO	JALISCO

▄▄ ▄ International Boundaries

– – – State Boundaries

Rivers

Major Transportation Routes

States Numbered on Map

1 AGUASCALIENTES   **5** TLAXCALA
2 GUANAJUATO   **6** MORELOS
3 QUERETARO   **7** MÉXICO
4 DISTRITO FEDERAL **8** PUEBLA

■ Guadalajara **Towns over 1,000,000**
● Tijuana **Towns over 100,000**
○ Laredo **Towns under 100,000**

Government

Mexico is a federal republic. It is made up of 31 states and Mexico City, which is a federal district much like Washington, DC. The president is elected by a direct vote of the citizens for a six-year term. The office of the president is very powerful, but he or she can only be elected to one term. The Congress is made up of two houses. The lower house is called the Chamber of Deputies. It is controlled by the ruling Institutional Revolutionary Party. The upper house, the Senate, has six parties.

A charter member of the United Nations, Mexico takes its role in the world community very seriously. The government takes consistent positions on international issues. It also opposes interference in the problems of other countries. It spends less than 10% of its budget on defence. By comparison the US spends over 60% on defence.

Mexico is a nonaligned country. This means that it treats international issues on their merits, and not on friendships with other countries. Mexico is unusual in its position among other Latin American countries. It is a post-revolutionary nation. Most of its neighbours, on the other hand, are in pre-revolutionary or revolutionary stages. It opposes all intervention in these countries, either from the United States or from Communist or other Latin American countries. Its votes in the United Nations have reflected these policies.

Currency

The Mexican *peso* and *centavo* are written as $ and ¢. The Mexican peso was once one of the most stable currencies in the world. Now the Mexican economy is very troubled, however, and its currency has lost much of its value.

Mexican currency.

Industry

Manufacturing industries have grown rapidly in Mexico. They make up 30% of all Mexican exports. Mexico's exports include crude oil, processed foods, chemicals, basic metals, metal products, rubber, and electric goods.

The factories along the US border are growing rapidly. These factories are known as *maquiladoras*. Here Mexican workers make products from American materials. These products are then sent back to be sold in the US. Eighteen percent of the Mexican labour force works in manufacturing.

Non-manufacturing industry includes Mexico's large tourism industry. Tourism provides jobs for many Mexicans, especially in the winter months.

Mexico City

Until 1325 the Aztecs had been a nomadic people. They then discovered the place promised them by their sun god, Huitzilopochtli: 'The land where an eagle perches on cactus leaves and holds a serpent in its beak is the land of prosperity'. An eagle holding a serpent in its beak: This is the central design of the Mexican flag.

The Aztecs built their capital on this land. They named it Tenochtitlán, which means 'alongside the cactus'. Spanish colonists later changed the name to Mexico City.

The metropolitan population of Mexico City is around 18 million. This means that Mexico City is today the world's second largest city. Thousands of Indians and mestizos arrive every day to live in the city, and the population grows by over 600,000 people a year. One sign of Mexico City's rapid growth is poverty and overcrowded living conditions. Mexico City has around five hundred slums. They are called *ciudades perdidas*, or lost cities. By the year 2000, experts predict that the population will be over 30 million.

A busy plaza near a train station in Mexico City.

Alongside the old buildings and the old culture are modern buildings, highways, and Underground railroads. Mexico City's traffic jams, pollution, and housing problems are matched by few cities anywhere. In many ways, however, its relaxed Latin pace of life still survives.

The centre of the city is a large square. Its official name is *Plaza de la Constitución* (Constitution Plaza) but it is known to everyone as the *Zócalo*. Here, at the National Palace, the president of Mexico strikes the bell at 11 p.m. on 15 September every year. He is joined by the crowds in Zócalo shouting 'Viva Mexico'! This begins the celebration of Mexico's independence from Spain.

Inside and around Mexico City the ancient culture of Mexico is seen in Aztec ruins and in museums, churches, and palaces. And yet the city is full of new things, such as the Latin American Tower. The tallest building in Mexico, it was designed by American architect Frank Lloyd Wright. Its foundation is made of floating chambers.

These chambers have helped the Latin American Tower resist Mexico City's frequent floods and earthquakes. Many other modern buildings in Mexico City were not so well-designed. They were among the hundreds of buildings destroyed in the earthquakes of 1985.

Mexico City: a modern metropolis sitting in a mountain valley, 2,100 m above sea level.

The Plaza of the Three Cultures is symbolic of present-day Mexico. Here are remains of Aztec temples and pyramids, Santiago Church from the colonial period, and ultramodern contemporary buildings.

The Underground, built jointly by the French and Mexican governments.

Another symbol of both the present and the past in Mexico City is the Underground system. Each station has its own symbol for those who can't read. While building the Pino Suárez station, workers discovered the remains of an Aztec temple. Now the station is a museum as well as an Underground stop. The bright orange cars ride on rubber-covered wheels. This makes them so quiet that music is piped into the stations.

Two earthquakes struck Mexico City on 19 and 20 September in 1985. These quakes did huge damage to a city where many people already lived in shanty towns and tents. In just two days, two large hospitals and four hundred office buildings were destroyed. Two hundred schools were damaged or destroyed. In all, more than eleven hundred buildings were badly damaged or destroyed. More than 31,000 people were left without homes. Within hours of the first quake, trained rescue teams from all over the world arrived in Mexico City to help search for survivors.

The patience and courage of the people of Mexico City provided moments of joy in the days following the tragedy. Eight days after the quakes, a newborn baby was found alive in the ruins of a hospital, and the whole world rejoiced.

Mexican Emigrants

Nearly 1,000 Mexicans live in the United Kingdom, including about 300 graduate and post graduate students at universities in Oxford, Cambridge and Manchester, mainly studying economics and science. The remainder are mostly businessmen concerned with trade, banking and the oil industry. It is estimated that about 2,000 Mexicans come to the UK on holiday each year especially to see the sights of London.

Glossary of Useful Mexican Terms

adios (ah-DYOS) .... good-bye
bebeleche (beh-beh-LAY-cheh) .... a hopscotch game
beisbol (BAZE-bol) .... baseball
carne (CAR-nay) .... meat
centavo..(sen-TAH-boh) .... cent
charreada (char-ray-AH-dah) .... rodeo
charro (CHAR-oh) .... a Mexian horseman who wears a special costume
chili (CHEE-lay) .... hot pepper
ciudad (syu-DAD) .... city (plural *ciudades* [syu-DAD-es])
corrido (cor-REE-doh) .... ballad; a song that tells a story
domingo (doh-MEEN-goh) .... Sunday
fiesta (fee-ES-tah) .... a festival or holiday
fútbol (FOOT-bol) .... soccer, Mexico's most popular sport
hacienda (ah-see-EN-dah) .... large farm or estate
¡hasta la vista! (AH-stah lah BEE-stah) .... good-bye!
jai-alai (HI-ah-li) .... a game played against a tall wall with a ball and hand-held basket
jugo (HU-goh) .... juice
libertad (lee-ber-TAD) .... liberty
mariachi (mah-ree-AH-chee) .... Mexican music and band typical of Guadalajara

matador (mah-tah-DOR) ....bullfighter who kills the bull
mejicano (meh-hee-CAHN-oh) ....Mexican
mestizos (mes-TEE-zos) ....people of mixed Spanish and Indian
background
mi (mee) ....my
muchas gracias (MU-chas GRAH-sias) ....thank you very much
no (no)..no
número (NU-meh-roh) ....number
pelota (peh-LOH-tah) ....the game of jai-alai; also, the ball
used in jai-alai
perdido (pare-DEE-doh) ....lost
peso (PEH-soh) ....unit of currency in some countries
pichón (peen-SHONE) ....pigeon
piñata (peen-YAH-tah) ....hanging pot filled with treats
pueblo (PWEH-bloh)..............................village
rey (rray) ....king (plural *reyes* [RRAY-es])
rosca (RROSE-kah)................................crown-shaped roll; circle
sangre (SAN-gray) ....blood
sí (see) ....yes
siesta (see-ES-tah) ....afternoon nap
sombrero (som-BRER-oh)......................hat
submarino (sube-mah-REE-noh) ....submarine
taco (TAH-coh) ....a folded tortilla sandwich
toreo (toh-RAY-oh)..............................bullfighting
torero (toh-RARE-oh) ....bullfighter
toro (TOH-roh)......................................bull
tortilla (tor-TEE-ah) ....a thin, toasted cake of cornmeal
tostada (tohs-TAH-dah) ....a kind of tortilla
zócalo (ZOH-cah-loh) ....public square

More Books About Mexico

Listed below are more books about Mexico. If you are interested in them, check
your library. You may find many of them helpful in doing research for some of the
'Things to Do' projects that follow.

Family in Mexico by P. O. Jacobsen & P. S. Kristensen (Wayland, 1984)
Let's Visit Mexico by J. C. Caldwell (Burke, 1984)
Mexico: Life in an Indian Village by P. Petersen (A. and C. Black, 1979)
Passport to Mexico by C. Irizarry (Franklin Watts, 1987)
We Live in Mexico by C. Somonte (Wayland, 1985)

Things to Do — Research Projects

Governments and economies change quickly. In the mid 1970s, for example, the
future looked very bright for Mexico because of its large supply of oil. In less than
ten years, however, the world's demand for oil had diminished. Mexico was

unable to sell its oil at the high prices it needed to continue the projects it had begun. Since 1982, the standard of living in Mexico has dropped 40%.

As you read about Mexico or any country, keep in mind the importance of having current information. Some of the research projects that follow need accurate, up-to-date information. That is why current newspapers and magazines are useful sources of information. Two publications your library may have will tell you about recent magazine and newspaper articles on many topics:

The Times Index
Keesing's Record of World Events

For accurate answers to questions about such topics of current interest as Mexico's earthquakes, economy, oil industry, and social and educational progress, look up *Mexico* in these two publications. They will lead you to the most up-to-date information you can find.

1. Some of the early Indian people of Mexico, such as the Toltecs, the Maya, and the Aztecs, developed great civilizations and became very powerful. Pick one of these peoples and do further research to learn more about their contributions to art, architecture, and science.

2. Draw two pictures that compare the architecture in two different ancient or modern Mexican civilizations.

3. How far is Guadalajara from where you live? Use maps, travel guides, travel agents, or any other resources you know of. Find out how you could get there and how long it would take.

4. Many rural Mexicans have moved to the cities in search of work and new opportunities. Thousands of mestizos and Indians come to Mexico City every day. Some have found prosperity. More have found worse poverty than they left.

Find the answers to these questions: Why have people moved to the cities? What must the cities have for this kind of movement to succeed? How does this situation compare with a movement, or migration, in your country?

5. Write a short report about a resource or industry important to Mexico.

6. Imagine that your parents decide to move to Mexico. They ask you which area you would like to live in. Investigate further about Mexico and pick a location. Give your reasons.

7. Pick a Mexican holiday that your country also celebrates. How do the two celebrations resemble each other? How are they different?

8. Look up *Mexico* in the *Times Index* or *Keesing's Record of World Events*. Find articles that have been written recently, and report to your classmates about what has been happening in the last few months.

More Things to Do — Activities

These projects are designed to encourage further thinking and talking about Mexico. They offer ideas and suggestions for interesting group or individual projects that you can do at school or at home.

1. Invite somebody from Mexico to visit your class to talk about his or her country. Prepare a list of interesting questions to ask.

2. How does your life compare with Elena's? Write a paragraph describing the ways in which you are the same or different.

3. If you were going to talk to a child from Mexico, what questions would you ask?

4. See if your class or another group you belong to wants to have a Mexican fiesta. You might want to have one for a birthday party. Decide what Mexican food you want to serve and dress in Mexican-style clothing. Your fiesta will look more like a real Mexican fiesta if you decorate the room.

5. If you would like a pen friend in Mexico, write to these people:

International Friendship League
Pen-Friend Service
Saltash
Cornwall

Friends by Post
6 Bollin Court, Macclesfield Road
Wilmslow
Cheshire

Be sure to tell them what country you want your pen friend to be from. Also, include your full name and address.

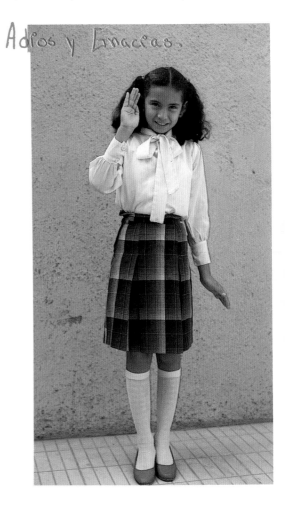

Index